This journal belongs to:

PLAN, DREAM, REFLECT

A THREE-YEAR PROGRESS JOURNAL

BY KATHARINE WATSON

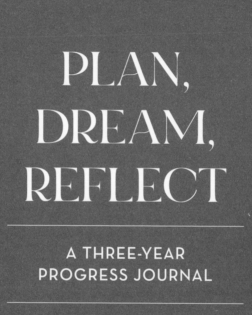

CHRONICLE BOOKS
SAN FRANCISCO

Let's stop and appreciate where we are today so we can plan where we want to go.

Everyone does it: We achieve a big goal or check something major off the to-do list, and then immediately plan for the next thing without taking time to reflect and feel proud. We don't allow ourselves to pause and notice how far we've come through incremental changes. And yet, it's a key part of goal setting to recognize how much progress you've already made.

Are you working on a big creative project, or embarking on a new chapter in your personal life? Are you learning a new skill, starting a new routine, or putting new habits into practice? The purpose of this journal is to allow you to stop and reflect. In these pages, you will take stock of your progress on projects and life changes from the past year and then set intentions for the year ahead. You might have seen the most change reflected in your daily life, or you might see the most change in the big picture—shifts in your goals and aspirations as you grow. In this journal, you'll take note of it all and ultimately create a memento that captures how far you've come.

I've been running my creative business for over a decade. When I started, I made a list of goals that I wanted to achieve in my artistic practice—from

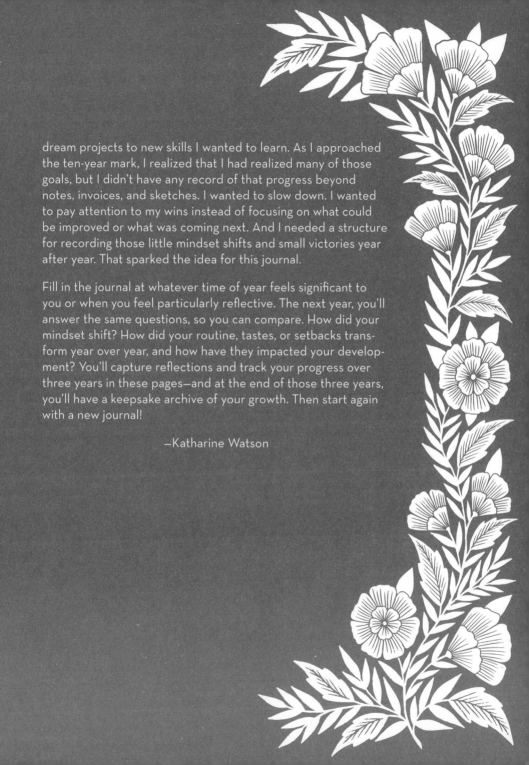

dream projects to new skills I wanted to learn. As I approached the ten-year mark, I realized that I had realized many of those goals, but I didn't have any record of that progress beyond notes, invoices, and sketches. I wanted to slow down. I wanted to pay attention to my wins instead of focusing on what could be improved or what was coming next. And I needed a structure for recording those little mindset shifts and small victories year after year. That sparked the idea for this journal.

Fill in the journal at whatever time of year feels significant to you or when you feel particularly reflective. The next year, you'll answer the same questions, so you can compare. How did your mindset shift? How did your routine, tastes, or setbacks transform year over year, and how have they impacted your development? You'll capture reflections and track your progress over three years in these pages—and at the end of those three years, you'll have a keepsake archive of your growth. Then start again with a new journal!

—Katharine Watson

YEAR ONE

LOOKING BACK:

REFLECTIONS ON THE LAST YEAR

My greatest achievement:

The biggest project I worked on:

A new skill I learned:

What has inspired me most:

How did I manage my time this year?

My typical daily routine:

An important relationship I made:

Five words I would use to describe my year:

1.

2.

3.

4.

5.

A story that most defines my year:

My greatest setback:

My biggest supporter:

The best advice I received:

What made this year unique?

What I'm most grateful for this year:

Who did I most enjoy spending time with?

My favorite place I went to this year:

My greatest area of growth:

What scared me?

Five things I feel proud of this year:

1.

2.

3.

4.

5.

My biggest learning experience this year:

Most delicious meal I ate:

_____

Favorite book of the year:

_____

Most-frequented restaurant:

_____

Favorite drink this year:

_____

Biggest purchase:

_____

Favorite way to relax:

_____

Most stunning view I saw:

_____

Favorite TV program or movie:

_____

Beloved item of clothing:

_____

An inside joke:

_____

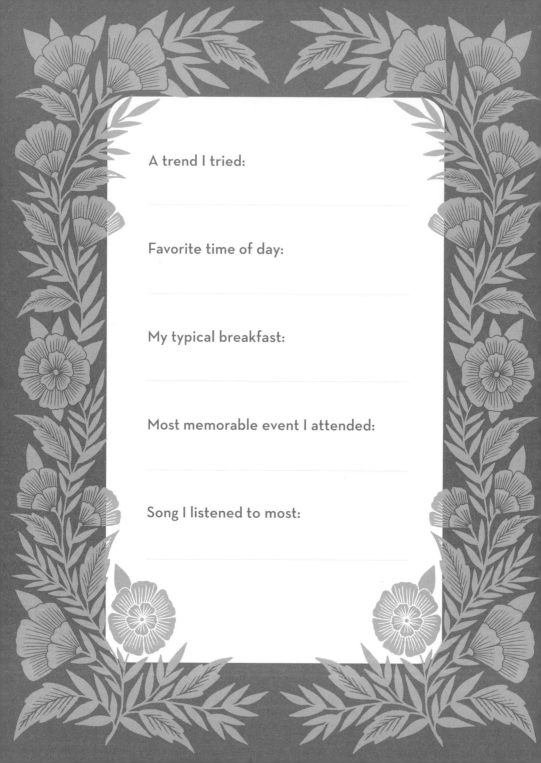

A trend I tried:

Favorite time of day:

My typical breakfast:

Most memorable event I attended:

Song I listened to most:

LOOKING AHEAD:

HOPES AND PLANS
FOR NEXT YEAR

The thing I'm most excited about:

Something I'm nervous about:

The biggest project I have coming up:

Something I want to change:

_____

_____

_____

_____

_____

_____

_____

_____

_____

_____

_____

Five things I would like to work on:

1.

2.

3.

4.

5.

An event I would like to participate in:

A place I would like to go:

A person I would like to connect with:

A habit I would like to change:

A new skill I hope to learn:

What do I want to do less of next year?

What do I want to do more of next year?

A key goal for next year:

Two steps I can take toward reaching that goal:

I'd like to set an intention to:

Five words I would use to describe my dreams for next year:

1.

2.

3.

4.

5.

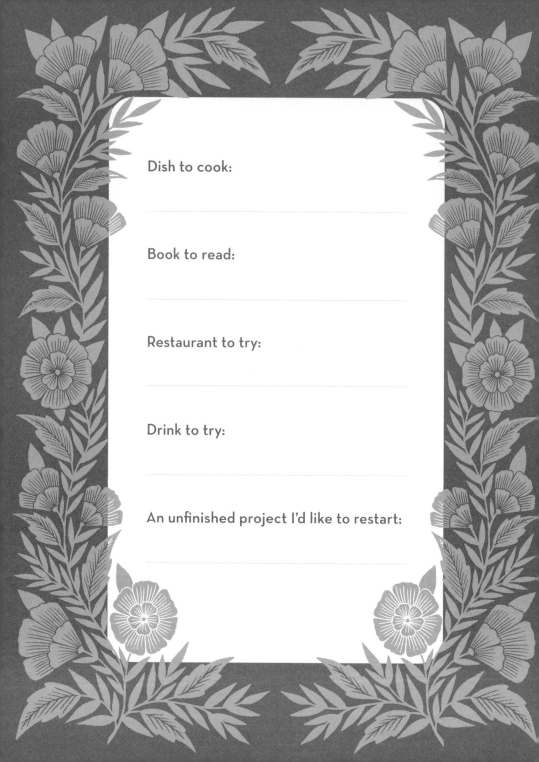

Dish to cook:

_____

Book to read:

_____

Restaurant to try:

_____

Drink to try:

_____

An unfinished project I'd like to restart:

_____

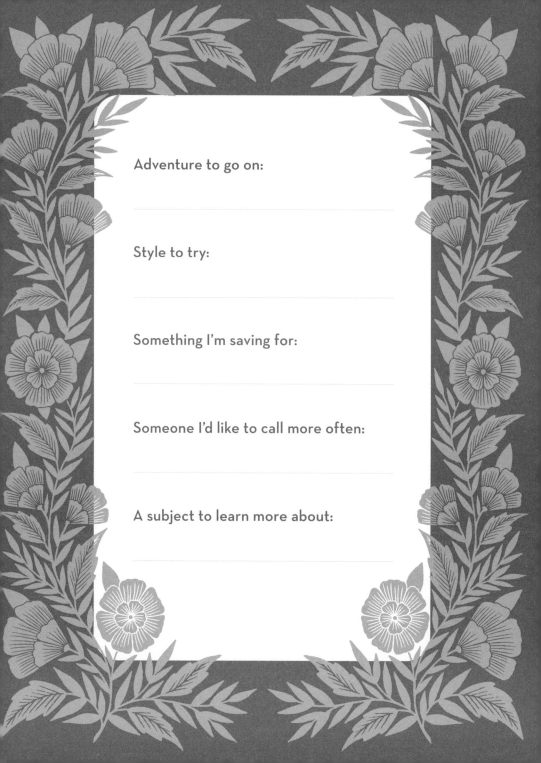

Adventure to go on:

Style to try:

Something I'm saving for:

Someone I'd like to call more often:

A subject to learn more about:

YEAR
TWO

LOOKING BACK:

REFLECTIONS
ON THE
LAST YEAR

My greatest achievement:

_____

_____

_____

_____

_____

_____

_____

_____

_____

_____

_____

_____

The biggest project I worked on:

A new skill I learned:

What has inspired me most:

How did I manage my time this year?

My typical daily routine:

An important relationship I made:

Five words I would use to describe my year:

1.

2.

3.

4.

5.

A story that most defines my year:

My greatest setback:

My biggest supporter:

The best advice I received:

What made this year unique?

What I'm most grateful for this year:

Who did I most enjoy spending time with?

My favorite place I went to this year:

My greatest area of growth:

What scared me?

Five things I feel proud of this year:

1.

2.

3.

4.

5.

My biggest learning experience this year:

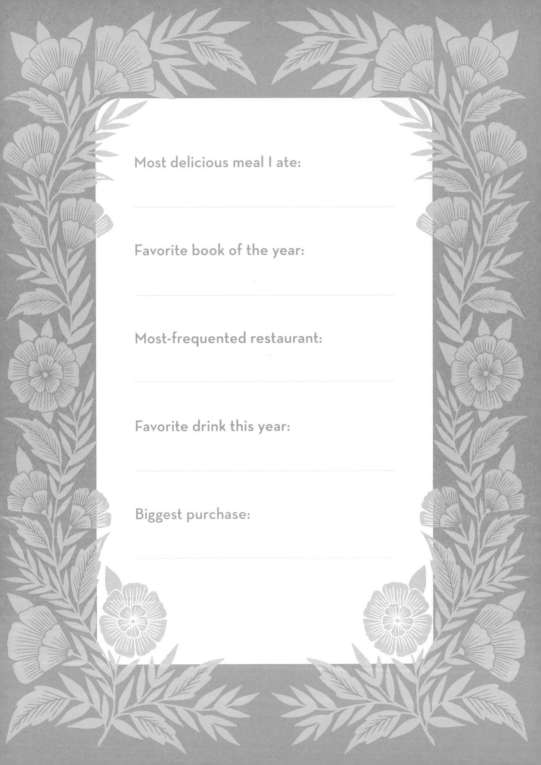

Most delicious meal I ate:

Favorite book of the year:

Most-frequented restaurant:

Favorite drink this year:

Biggest purchase:

Favorite way to relax:

_____

Most stunning view I saw:

_____

Favorite TV program or movie:

_____

Beloved item of clothing:

_____

An inside joke:

_____

A trend I tried:

_____

Favorite time of day:

_____

My typical breakfast:

_____

Most memorable event I attended:

_____

Song I listened to most:

_____

LOOKING AHEAD:

HOPES AND PLANS
FOR NEXT YEAR

The thing I'm most excited about:

Something I'm nervous about:

The biggest project I have coming up:

Something I want to change:

Five things I would like to work on:

1.

2.

3.

4.

5.

An event I would like to participate in:

A place I would like to go:

A person I would like to connect with:

A habit I would like to change:

A new skill I hope to learn:

What do I want to do less of next year?

What do I want to do more of next year?

A key goal for next year:

Two steps I can take toward reaching that goal:

I'd like to set an intention to:

Five words I would use to describe my dreams for next year:

1.

2.

3.

4.

5.

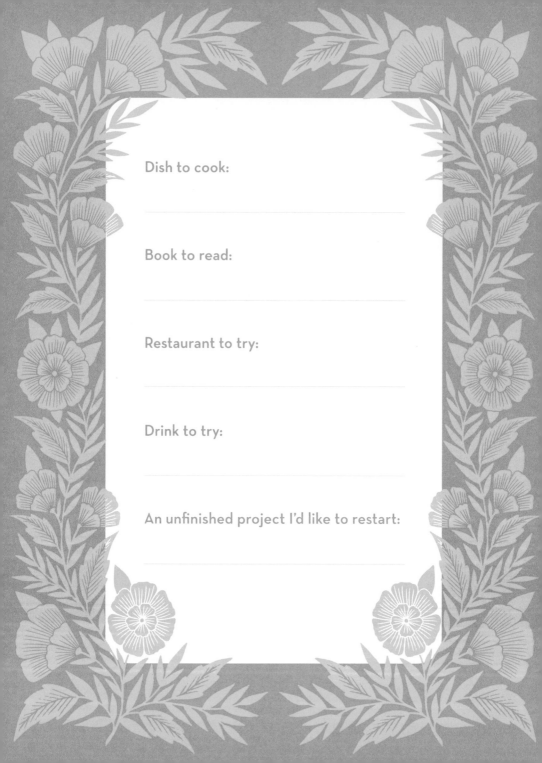

Dish to cook:

_____

Book to read:

_____

Restaurant to try:

_____

Drink to try:

_____

An unfinished project I'd like to restart:

_____

Adventure to go on:

Style to try:

Something I'm saving for:

Someone I'd like to call more often:

A subject to learn more about:

YEAR
THREE

LOOKING BACK:

REFLECTIONS ON THE LAST YEAR

My greatest achievement:

_____

_____

_____

_____

_____

_____

_____

_____

_____

_____

_____

_____

_____

_____

_____

The biggest project I worked on:

A new skill I learned:

What has inspired me most:

How did I manage my time this year?

My typical daily routine:

An important relationship I made:

Five words I would use to describe my year:

1.

2.

3.

4.

5.

A story that most defines my year:

My greatest setback:

My biggest supporter:

The best advice I received:

What made this year unique?

What I'm most grateful for this year:

Who did I most enjoy spending time with?

My favorite place I went to this year:

My greatest area of growth:

What scared me?

Five things I feel proud of this year:

1.

2.

3.

4.

5.

My biggest learning experience this year:

Most delicious meal I ate:

_____

Favorite book of the year:

_____

Most-frequented restaurant:

_____

Favorite drink this year:

_____

Biggest purchase:

_____

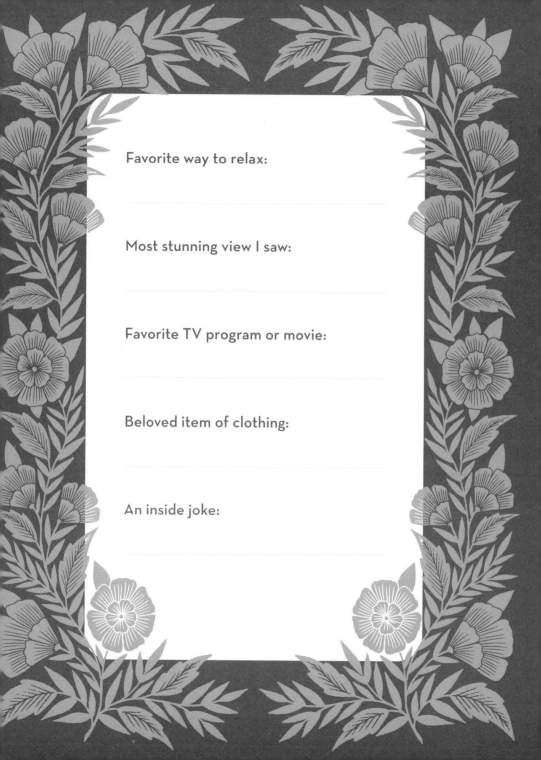

Favorite way to relax:

Most stunning view I saw:

Favorite TV program or movie:

Beloved item of clothing:

An inside joke:

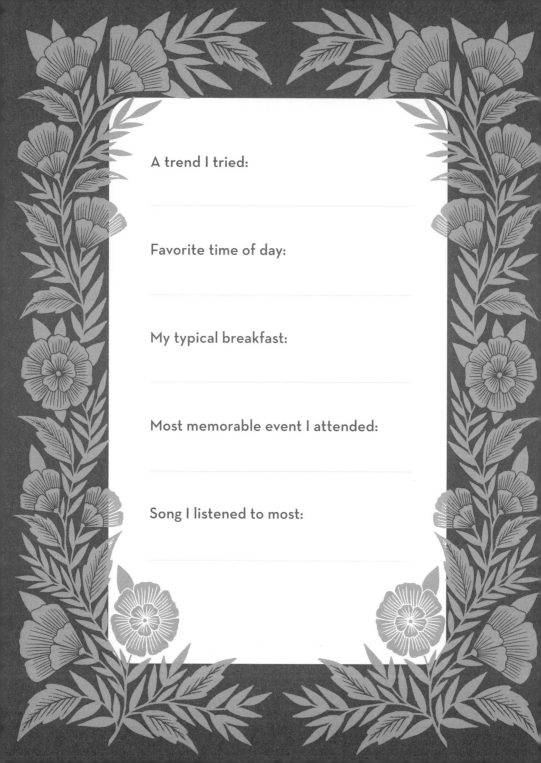

A trend I tried:

Favorite time of day:

My typical breakfast:

Most memorable event I attended:

Song I listened to most:

LOOKING AHEAD:
HOPES AND PLANS
FOR NEXT YEAR

The thing I'm most excited about:

Something I'm nervous about:

The biggest project I have coming up:

Something I want to change:

_____

_____

_____

_____

_____

_____

_____

_____

_____

_____

_____

Five things I would like to work on:

1.

2.

3.

4.

5.

An event I would like to participate in:

A place I would like to go:

A person I would like to connect with:

A habit I would like to change:

A new skill I hope to learn:

What do I want to do less of next year?

What do I want to do more of next year?

A key goal for next year:

Two steps I can take toward reaching that goal:

I'd like to set an intention to:

Five words I would use to
describe my dreams for next year:

1.

2.

3.

4.

5.

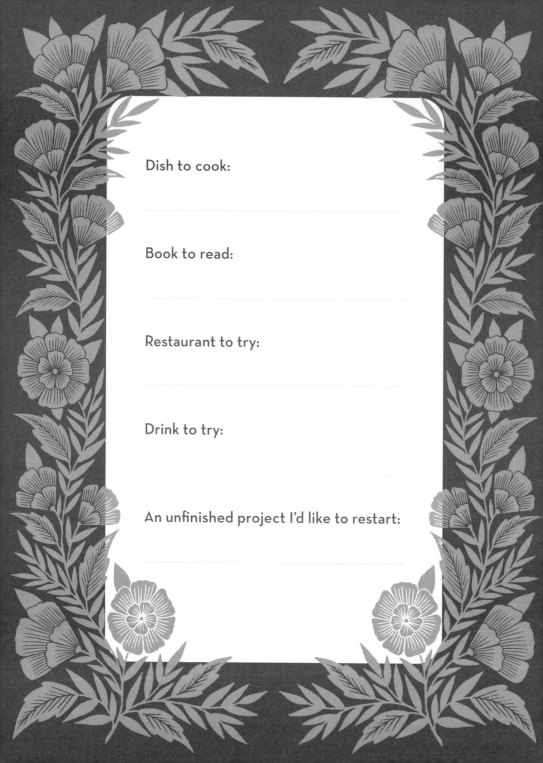

Dish to cook:

Book to read:

Restaurant to try:

Drink to try:

An unfinished project I'd like to restart:

Adventure to go on:

Style to try:

Something I'm saving for:

Someone I'd like to call more often:

A subject to learn more about:

Katharine Watson hand-carves, prints, and paints her designs from her studio in Portland, Maine. Through her eponymous brand launched in 2009, she produces prints, textiles, ceramics, and paper goods featuring her artwork that are carried in stores internationally. She is the artist behind the *Rose Gold Notebooks* and *Rose Gold Notecards*, also from Chronicle Books. See more Katharine Watson gift products at www.chroniclebooks.com.

ISBN 978-1-7972-0070-5

Manufactured in China.
Art by Katharine Watson.
Design by Kristen Hewitt.

10 9 8 7 6 5 4 3 2 1

Chronicle Books publishes distinctive books and gifts. From award-winning children's titles, bestselling cookbooks, and eclectic pop culture to acclaimed works of art and design, stationery, and journals, we craft publishing that's instantly recognizable for its spirit and creativity. Enjoy our publishing and become part of our community at www.chroniclebooks.com.

Special quantity discounts are available to corporations and other organizations. Contact our premiums department at corporatesales@chroniclebooks.com or at 1-800-759-0190.

Chronicle Books LLC
680 Second Street
San Francisco, California 94107
www.chroniclebooks.com